NOTHING IS FREE:

RESOLVE THE NATIONAL DEBT

M. S. Platt

Copyright ©2019 by M. S. Platt

ISBN: 9781795502412

All rights are reserved. Portions of this book may be reviewed, but a citation must be given.

This book was printed in the United States of America. To order additional copies of this book, contact: Amazon.com

TABLE OF CONTENTS

Preface — Page 3
Chapter 1: The Financial Crisis. The Debt — Page 8
Chapter 2: Dealing with the Rising Cost — Page 11
Chapter 3: The Tax Burden on Taxpayers — Page 16
Chapter 4: Epilogue — Page 19

PREFACE

The destruction of a nation. Multiple characters are accountable. They serve as Putin's accomplices. Together all of these will destroy freedom and the Constitution in our land.

This is NO idyll dream. Look at the FACTS:

There is a financial crisis in our Federal Treasury. The National debt grows each day and undermines our commerce and financial credibility. Look at the facts of the 2019 fiscal budget. Consider the revenue and expenses. Expenses are growing due to increased mandatory spending. The elderly people in our population are increasing, and mandatory spending will increase for the next 40-60 years. The National debt will constantly increase. The cost of paying the debt will increase. Those who lend to the United States will refuse to carry our debt, and the nation becomes bankrupt. Indeed, unless we buckle down, we will become bankrupt.

The financial health of the nation is being destroyed in favor of abundant wealth of the few while the many suffer from pay check to paycheck (the workers who live by weekly paychecks; the elderly who rely on monthly Social Security paychecks.) You are absolutely vulnerable. Look at your personal, family financial situations. Are you immune?

Putin dances in his shoes. For he has won the Cold War. A Cold War that he has never relinquished, and now in which he takes the superior position. He has made some people in our government accomplices who try to take control of our Constitution and Congress.

Putin has aligned with the Middle East nations so that our alliances with our allies are now untrustworthy, and Isis and Taliban succeed while our troops are compromised. Putin has aligned Iran with the Saudis. He allows the Arab petroleum block to gain dominance of our markets. Our national financial policies weaken our moral and financial structures. We give in to the greedy and money interests, and they become empowered over the weak and meek.

Our religious-right parties hold the Bible as their guide, not recognizing that their position is immoral and Antichrist. These people believe in Christ, yet seek to undermine the love of God, --of fellow neighbors--and in all that Jesus taught us. The love of MONEY is the root of our evil. This is what Paul and the Disciples taught us. Yet we do not heed this sermon. We cause confrontations between rich and poor yet do not seek the love that should bind us.

We are weak in spirit and will. We have a terrible narcotic abuse crisis, but we do nothing to help these people deal with it. We have no health programs or national service commitments by the young people in our society. We do not have a strong military although we spend excess funds to maintain it. The few serve the many. We do not have universal military training for all of our youth, nor do we demand civil service duty by all the people—the young and elderly. In the 1940's, we were alert enough to prepare for World War II, but today, we do not have the will or preparation to do so. We have no real defenses against Chinese or Russian aggression or trade. They will succeed in undermining us by creating vast trade imbalances. Our nation's greed for luxuries and toys will lead us to constant negative trade balances, debt, and financial disarray. Then our creditors will undermine us by calling up the debt that is due, and we will need to declare bankruptcy.

Where is our honor, our "esprit de corps"---our "noblesse oblige"-- our desire to serve the Nation, our Constitution?

Our infrastructure is in chaos. Our electrical grid, roads and bridges are dysfunctional and in disrepair. Our social networks are open to interference and designed to work against our privacy interests and our financial resources.

Our television presentations are nothing but one advertisement after another. These invite us to spend money we do not have, more debt we do not need, and more greed for luxuries that will never make us truly happy. Where is the love of our Lord, the love of our neighbors that guided us through the millennia?

Isolationism and nationalism may be the protective stance of the day, but the nation forgets that intercontinental missiles and rapid, high-speed jet traffic preclude those notions. Any single country with ambition and weaponry can threaten another or the planet, and all of us must now recognize that if we don't stand together, we will all hang together (as Benjamin Franklin advised the signers at the Declaration of Independence.)

Global economics is the matter at hand here. It is well discussed in Holy Economics on pages 88-93. Economies function because of economic advantages of one country in relation to another, and one country buys and sells based on those advantages. China will sell goods to the United States because it has a lower cost of production. Thus, the United States must learn to buy selectively before it outgrows its capacity to spend and borrow, and eventually become bankrupt. That is the nature of economics, and the United States must learn that lesson. This nation will not be in a position to sell its goods to the world as it did in World War I and World War II. In fact, it is now a borrower nation like Europe was in those wars. The United States can use tariffs to control its borrowing capacity, but it would be better if it used bilateral reciprocal trade policies to balance its trade deficits and maintain some degree of economic wealth and health (as described in *Holy Economics* on pages 88-93.)

Those who understand what I teach will assist in repairing this nation. Those who misunderstand will destroy me and my kind. They will crucify me on a "Cross of Gold" as they did to Jesus.

How can the United States avert this catastrophe? I offer a financial pathway for success. May the Lord guide me in this endeavor. Everyone must contribute. The poor as much as the wealthy must contribute, in hand as well as in money. Contribution must be the model of behavior. FOR NOTHING IS FREE.

Chapter 1: The Financial Crisis-The Debt

In 2019, the national debt reached $21 -$22 trillion. In order to understand how this happened, one must understand how the federal debt arises and how the federal budget operates. According to the Constitution, the Congress of the United States passes a budget each year. When it spends more than its income (its revenue), it needs to borrow this deficit.

Since the late 1970's the federal government has increased it's debt. This was especially seen during the 2008 to 2010 recession and when liberal tax laws were passed such as in 2018.

The budget process of 2019 is a case in point. The income (revenues) projected in 2019 is estimated to be $3.422 trillion. The expenses (the spending/expenditures) for 2019 is estimated to be $4.407 trillion. Since the nation spends more than it receives, it must borrow the difference. This difference adds to the total debt. In 2019, it is estimated that the federal treasury will need to borrow $985 billion ($3.422 trillion minus $4.407 trillion.) The total debt will amount to $21- $22 trillion. Almost 40% of this debt is owned by foreign investors.

One may ask, where does the income come from? Individual taxpayers will contribute about $1.684 trillion. Payroll taxes from Social Security taxes and from Medicare add $1.238 trillion. Other sources of income are from corporation taxes

($225 billion), excise/tariff taxes ($152 billion), estate taxes ($68 billion) and federal reserve investments ($55 billion). Thus, the total income amounts to $3.422 trillion.

The expenditures are another matter. The cost to borrow the 2019 $985 billion deficit and pay the $22 trillion debt amounts to $363 billion. These will rise because the debt is rising. Then, there are discretionary expenditures. These are necessary to run the government. These include the cost of the military, government offices such as the State Department, Transportation, Veterans Department, Homeland Security, NASA, etc. In 2019, $1.307 trillion was allocated for discretionary expenditures.

In addition, this country faces increasing costs for mandatory expenses and social needs. It will do so because the country's population is increasing and aging. This is a fact that cannot be denied or dismissed. In addition, there will be times when recessions and wars will require emergency spending. The deficits and debt may then increase. How will it be possible to meet these demands? I suggest that it is possible, but this nation will need to change its direction, its philosophy, and its taxing procedures in order to do this. In addition, it will need to adjust its social philosophy so as to care for its meek, its weak, its poor---for these are the ones who account for most of its economy, its status, its population, its military in time of crisis. (see *"A Simplified Tax Structure for the United States"*, pages 8-9.)

In addition to its rising health costs, there will be social needs that will need to be met. These cannot be met by decreasing mandatory expenditures, for the country will continue to grow, and its population will need support in that growth. Cutting costs will not work as shown in *"The Myth: Soak the Rich", pages 6-8.* And the wealthy will need to understand how American capitalism works in this country. They should heed the advice rendered in *"A Simplified Structure for the United States (pp. 8-9) and "The Myth: Soak the Rich, page 11.* A rendition of these social needs and costs include: Job support in times of recession ($280 billion/year), help in college tuition ($75 billion/year), infrastructure (tax on gasoline and road use), and maternity leave. Support for these social functions are described in *The Myth: Soak the Rich, pages 27-30.*

There will be a need to develop a health care program "for a nation that is physically, mentally, and emotionally ill cannot survive the rigors of 21st Century life." (see *Holy Economics*, page 62 and *The Myth, page 25*). A plan to deal with this rising demand will be described in Chapter 2.

Chapter 2: Dealing with the rising costs of the Budget

Domenici and Rivlin suggested two plans in 2010 (citation available.) These would reduce the debt. The first was based on a consumption or VAT tax. Because there was resistance to a VAT tax at that time, a Domenici-Rivlin Plan 2 was suggested. Unfortunately, neither plan was adopted, and the National Debt continued to rise without abatement. I propose several measures to deal with the social needs of this nation:

1. Social Security costs—See *Holy Economics,* pp.42-43. Several pathways have been suggested to increase the Social Security Trust Fund. Congress could raise the retirement age to 68 by 2050 and 69 by 2075. In the alternative, Congress could raise the taxable maximum for the Social Security payroll tax to $200,000 or $300,000.
2. Health Issues—See *Holy Economics*, pp 62-80, especially the summary at pp. 79-80.
    a. Health care should be covered for all persons domiciled in the United States. Combine Medicare, Medicaid, Child Care, and dental care for all.
    b. Develop a Health Care Fund. Initiate a VAT tax or sales/consumption tax on all goods and services. A 10% tax on these would raise about $1.8 trillion. That is the amount as suggested in *The Myth: Soak the Rich,* pp. 24-27, pp. 32-33, and pp. 36-38. Transfer the income from this tax to the states in proportion to their populations

such that state-wide corporations could administer state citizen-owned shareholder health care (see *Holy Economics*, pp. 62-80.) Provide for state citizen voting in these corporations so that they can develop health plans to their liking but limiting costs compatible with their financial circumstances. When income transferred by the federal government is less than the costs for services rendered to state citizens, then these states can impose increased taxes on their citizens, or the citizens can vote to limit or curtail some of the services offered to them (see *Holy Economics,* p.80.) Some observers dislike VAT or consumption taxes (citation available.) They claim that VAT taxes amount to a hidden tax, that these taxes will be competitive with state and local consumption taxes, that they give too much power to governments who will raise the taxes, that these taxes invite an underground economy or fraud, and that they are regressive. Some of these objections can be ameliorated by limiting the tax to health needs only, setting a limit on the federal tax distribution so that states carry some of the tax burden, and offering a federal deduction of $1000- $2000 to all taxpayers with incomes under $100,000 annually. This deduction would serve in place of not taxing groceries or some other product.

c. Develop team-oriented health care as described in *Holy Economics*, pp. 66-69. These teams would limit fraud and excess spending by health-care givers.

d. Limit medical litigation as suggested in *Holy Economics,* pp. 78-80.
   e. Limit excessive drug costs by developing state-funded cooperatives in competition with aggressive drug companies.
   f. Use Medicare-type payment schedules similar to those used by Medicare and the State of Maryland.

3. Offer a jobs program for all who wish to work as described in *Holy Economics,* pp.83-87.
4. Develop a National Service Corp as described in *Holy Economics,* pp. 86-87. The Service Corp program would deal with the health needs and drug/narcotic abuse of the youths of our nation.
5. Offer College tuition support. This would require $75 billion/year and is described in *The Myth: Soak the Rich* at pages 28-30.
6. Offer infrastructure improvements as described in *The Myth: Soak the Rich* on pages 27-28. The financing of this program must come from a gasoline and road use tax. A driver of a regular auto would pay $150/year if the auto is driven about 14,000 miles per year. Truck drivers or their owners would pay a tax of about $560 per year. In addition, all drivers who use a freeway or interstate roads would pay 1 cent a mile for use. Their autos or trucks would have an electronic tag that would identify the vehicle similar to turnpike EZ passes (but could not be used to identify the person in any government

investigations.) The income from these sources would allocate more than $1 trillion annually.
7. Medical leave support. A federal or state-wide insurance corporation would utilize a 2% tax on those who would pay for premiums for this service.

Would the revenue funds achieved in 2019 support these expenditures? What are the expenditures?

Social Security, as amended, would be self-supporting.
Health Care would be self-supporting.
Jobs program cost--$280 billion annually, if needed. All who wish, can work. There would be no poverty, if social programs are planned properly. This is not Socialism; it is community caring.
College tuition program cost--$75 billion annually.
Infrastructure program—self-supporting. Persons who use the roads, the bridges, the electrical grids, etc. need to contribute to support them.
Medical leave program—self-supporting.
Discretionary spending--$1,307 billion ($1.307 trillion).
Reduction of the National debt--$500 to $1000 billion annually returned to the Treasury or to pay off any debts owed to foreign investors. By law, these sums must be used for debt reduction only and not for any additional services.

THESE EXPENSE ITEMS amount to $2,662 to $3,162 billion annually. The REVENUE is $3,422 billion. This is cost effective.

The National Debt could be markedly diminished within 10 to 20 years. Since it took 20 years to form this debt, the outcome is successful, and the nation's finances are saved. Let us hope that the nation's moral fiber is saved.

As an aside, it is possible to reduce corporation taxes to 10% if corporations agree to serve the nation (as described in *Holy Economics,* pp. 55-56. By using these social contract agreements, a "territorial system" (as described in *Holy Economics)* and the use of a 10% competitive rate, this country could invite foreign corporations to incorporate within the United States and employ more U.S. citizens. There may be a loss of $171 billion in revenue, but this sum is still covered by the 2018 revenues and would develop more trade and business in the country.

CHAPTER 3: The tax burden on individuals.

A question arises: Will these tax suggestions burden the taxpayer? The answer is that they will not be burdened in 2018-2019 (when a new tax law took effect) when compared to tax year 2016 (when the latest data was available). I will share these data in this Chapter briefly and will also make the details available to any readers who communicate with me by e-mail (plattmsp@gmail.com). Any references noted in this publication will also be available at this address.

In 2018, the tax law was changed. The standard deduction was increased to $12,000, but the personal exemption was discontinued. In 2016, the deduction for a single taxpayer was $6300 and the personal exemption was $4050 (a total deduction of $10,350.)

The tax burden is related to income level. The Federal income levels are described by the Internal Revenue Service. They can be grouped arbitrarily as:

The very poor: income less than $20,000 annually.
The poor: income from $20,001 to $40,000 annually.
Middle class: income from $40,001 to $100,000 annually.
Professionals: income from $100,001 to $200,000/year.
Wealthy: income from $200,001 to $500,000/year.
Very wealthy: income in excess of $500,000/year.

Some of the taxes that are imposed on taxpayers are federal income taxes. These range from 10% to 37% and are based on the taxable income of the taxpayer. Taxable income is income minus any deductions or credits. For single persons in 2018, the tax was 10% for taxable income less than $9500, 12% for income $9500 to $38,700, 22% for income $38,700 to $82,500, 24% for income $82,500 to $157,500, 32% for income $157,500 to $200,000, 35% for income $200,000 to $500,000 and 37% for income greater than $500,000. There are also federal payroll taxes of 6.2% for social security and 1.45% for Medicare (total 7.65%.) Taxpayers are also subject to state income taxes that range from 3% to 10% depending on the state. The suggested health tax would subject them to taxes that could range from 6% to 10% depending on their income level. Property and state sales taxes are state specific and are not part of this analysis.

What is the total burden of these taxes on single taxpayers?

In 2016, the total tax on the very poor would have been 20.5-25.5% of their income, the poor at 20.5-26.5%, the middle class at 26.5-37.5% (the latter at an income of $100,000), professionals at 35-38%, the wealthy at 36-51%, and very wealthy at 51%. In 2018, these single persons would have been taxed at rates of the very poor at 25.2%, poor at 25.2-27.2%, middle class at 28.2-41.2%, professionals at 43-52%, wealthy at 52-55%, and very wealthy at 57%. Note that the rates for 2018 would also include the 10% Health tax.

Here are a few examples for these calculations:

For the very poor, 2016: Fed IRS-10%, Payroll tax -7.5%, State income tax-3%----total 20.5%.

For the very poor, 2019: Fed IRS-10%, Health Tax 6%, Social Security only-6.2%, State income tax-3%----total 25.2%.

Data to support the other findings are available upon request. Note that the rates described for 2016 and for 2018 are comparable except for an increased tax of about 5% (not 10%) to pay for the Health Tax.

CHAPTER 4: Epilogue.

The national debt is now $21 to $22 trillion and counting. Unless we change our ways, it is bankruptcy and dissolution of our Union, our Nation. Note that Socrates, in The *Republic*, (citation available) predicted that democracies would not survive. The citizens of democracies seek ultimate freedom, such that the lower classes grow larger and larger. Then those people choose to do whatever they want, but their desires lead them ultimately to a state of anarchy. We, in this Nation, need to prove Socrates wrong.

As noted in *Holy Economics,* at page *95,* this country prevailed during the Civil War, the Depression, and World War II. It needs to prevail now. It will take hard work and demands on its citizens, but this nation can succeed as it did before. As President Lincoln said at his first inaugural address, "we must not be enemies. Though passion may have strained, it must not break the bounds of affection. The mystic bonds of memory...all over this broad land will yet swell the chorus of Union, when again touched, as surely they will be, by the better angels of our nature."

We must continue to believe that this country is a wonderful country, a great country; that it has redemptive qualities and resiliency such that it will deal with its external and internal tensions and succeed. Somehow it got off its track and veered into troublesome waters, but this crisis is manageable. It requires will. We govern by the rule of law, not by anarchy.

Anarchy is chaos and is a form of treason to the Constitution and the mind-set of the Nation. "We pray that this Nation, under God, shall have a new birth of freedom---and that government of the people, by the people, for the people, shall not perish from this earth" (Lincoln, Gettysburg Address, 1863).

We can live within our means. We must live within our means, and in doing so, we must avoid the hills and valleys of our economy, the booms and busts that disrupt it. We are faced in this time of our history to change again, within Constitutional bounds, to overcome our fiscal, economic, and moral dilemmas. In our past history, those who were the land gentry, those who became the business aristocracy, took on the duty to lead the nation. Where is our land gentry now? Where is our "noblesse obliges" today? Where will it come from? We must educate and economically support our youth so that they can come up the ranks to serve as they did in prior times.

Yes. We have a capitalistic society, but we need a caring, capitalistic society. We have always had a cooperative society, not a socialist society. The mind-set of this nation balances the interests of its members to seek justice and is framed by our ancestors who recognized the beauty, the strength of community. We, in the community, have a social contract with ourselves, our neighbors, our government. In that strength we have grown to be a great force in the nations of this earth. Pray that we shall remain to do so.

Other publications by the author:

Do Not Forsake Me, Martin Luther King, Jr.-The Uncertainty of His American Dream. (2007 and 2012).

Holy Economics: Resolving the Debt Crisis. (2011).

A Simplified Tax Structure for the United States. (2015).

The Myth: Soak the Rich. (2015).

The Last Supper. (2016).

All in the Name of God. (2018).

These are available from Amazon.com

www.ingramcontent.com/pod-product-compliance
Lightning Source LLC
Chambersburg PA
CBHW071204220526
45468CB00003B/1157